Ripley's Believe It or Not!®

ZANY PUZZLE BOOK

In this Zany Puzzle Book you'll battle through mighty mazes, join the dots, and spot differences in pictures that at first look the same.

BUT STOP!

This is no ordinary puzzle book!

At Ripley's Believe It or Not! we celebrate the extraordinary side of life. This book is packed with some of the curious creatures, amazing art and freaky food that make up our wonderful world—and each page comes with a Ripley weird story!

RIPLEY
PUBLISHING

a Jim Pattison Company

INCREDIBLE EDIBLE

A birthday cake is always special but none more so than this giant chocolate and vanilla dragon cake made by one artistic baker!

Follow the wiggly paths to see which child gets to munch on the delicious birthday treat below.

SPORTS MAD

Believe it or not, American Bruce Crevier spun a single basketball on his fingers for over 22 hours!

Can you fill in the grid with the sports words listed so they all fit?

4 LETTERS
GOLF

6 LETTERS
SOCCER
TENNIS

7 LETTERS
CRICKET
SKATING
SURFING

8 LETTERS
FOOTBALL
BASEBALL

F

Answers on page 30

Answers on page 30

FUNNY RACE

At the "Down the Hill" race in Mexico, competitors have to go through a house! They go in through a door, down a flight of stairs, and out through another door.

What are they racing on?
Write in the letters from the colored squares to reveal the answer.

The answer is a

BRILLIANT BALLOONS

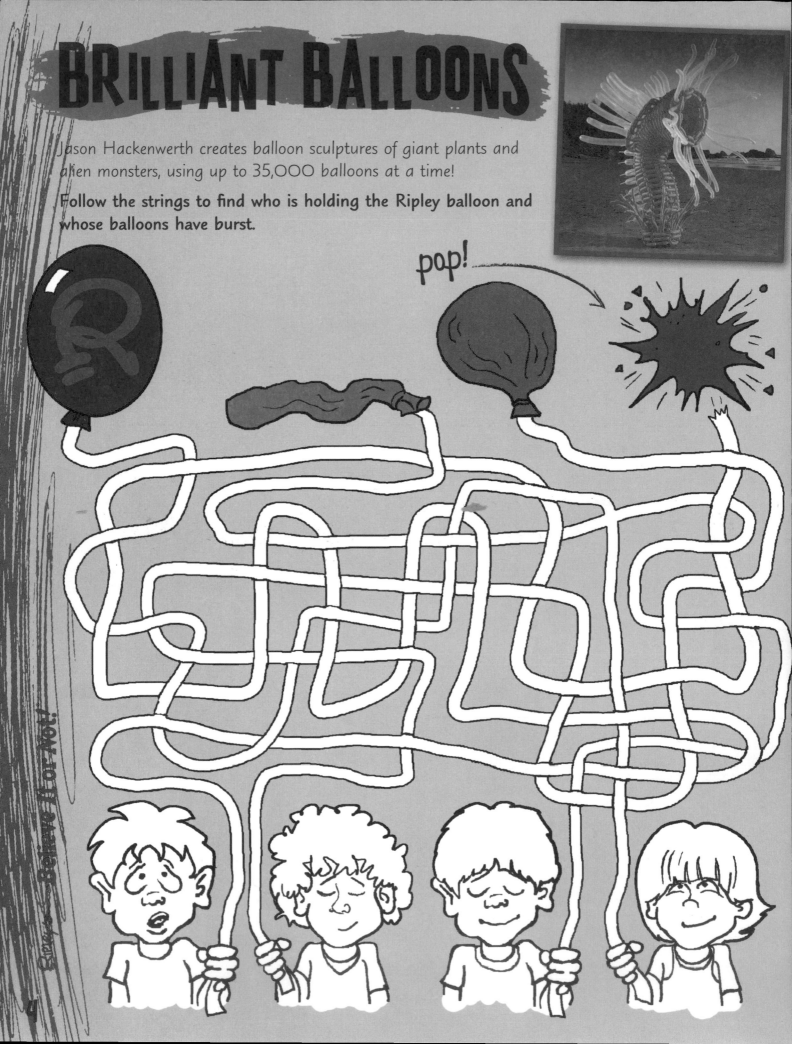

Jason Hackenwerth creates balloon sculptures of giant plants and alien monsters, using up to 35,000 balloons at a time!

Follow the strings to find who is holding the Ripley balloon and whose balloons have burst.

pop!

HOMER'S D'OH-NUT

A giant doughnut made from 90,000 regular doughnuts was made in Australia to celebrate the release of *The Simpsons Movie*. Believe it or not, it weighed the same as two rhinoceroses!

Find your way through the maze to get to the finger-licking good doughnut.

Answer on page 30

PECKER PUZZLE

Discover the story behind this picture by solving the number code.
Each number matches a letter in the grid below, but some of the spaces are
blank, so you'll have to work out what the missing letters might be!

Match each number to the correct letter and write
the letter underneath. Answer on page 30.

22 3 6 16 12 1 6 22 1 22

8 24 7 12 5   1 26 9 1

26 7 12 10 15 21   23 24 24 5 17 16 3 4 16 15 22

26 9 5   17 16 3 4 16 5   24 18 16 15   **200**

26 24 2 16 22   6 12   1 26 16   8 24 9 11

6 12 22 7 2 9 1 6 24 12   24 12   1 26 16   22 17 9 3 16

22 26 7 1 1 2 16   5 6 22 3 24 18 16 15 21 ' 22

8 7 16 2   1 9 12 4   22 24   9   12 9 22 9

23 24 15 4 16 15   20 24 7 10 26 1   **6**   17 2 9 22 1 6 3

24 23 2 22   1 24   22 3 9 15 16   1 26 16 11   9 23 9 21

A	B	C	D	E	F	G	H	I	J	K	L	M
	20	3	5	16	8	10	26	6	13	4	2	11

N	O	P	Q	R	S	T	U	V	W	X	Y	Z
12		17	19		22	1		18	23	25	21	14

COOL PENGUINS

Why are these cute penguins wearing sweaters? Well, in 2011, knitters around the world were asked to make woolly warmers for penguins affected by a big oil spill in the sea near New Zealand! The sweaters stopped the penguins from eating the oil in their feathers.

Follow the threads to discover which ball of wool made which sweater. Then color in the balls to match.

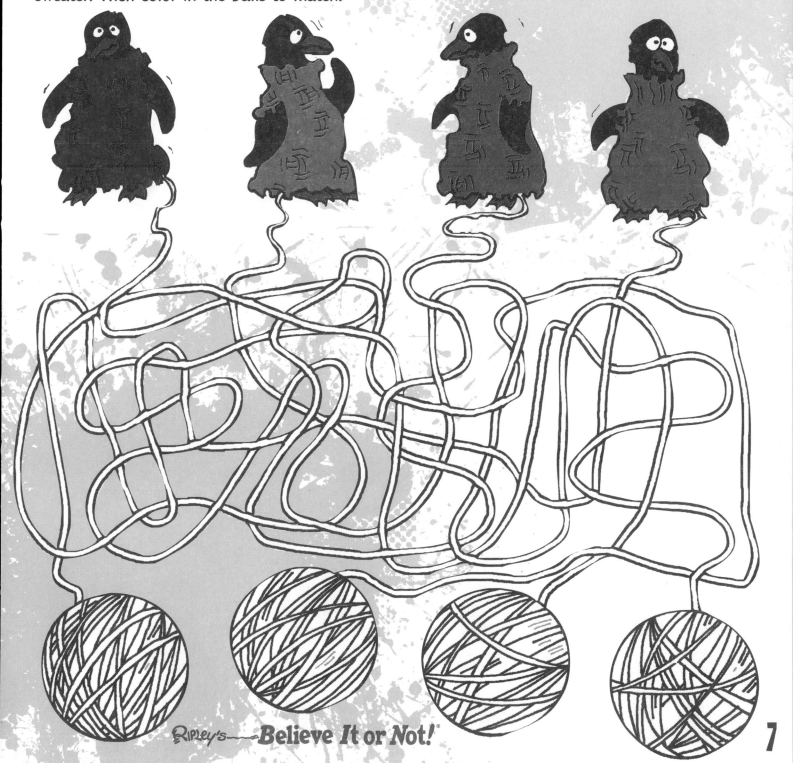

BRUSH UP!

American dentist Dr. Val Kolpakov's unbelievably large collection of toothpaste includes some peculiar flavors such as curry and bamboo!

How many types of toothpaste does he have? Cross out the pairs of numbers on the brushes to leave the correct answer. Check if you are right on page 30.

CRAZY CAT CIRCUS

Roll up, roll up, to Yuri Kuklachev's Moscow Cats Theater, and see amazing housecats perform all kinds of tricks from tightrope-walking to handstands!

Can you spot the 10 differences in the circus scenes below?

Answers on page 30

This naughty mouse has sneaked into the bottom picture. Can you find him?

ON THE MOVE

However much you love your pets, sometimes they get themselves into sticky situations...

Find out what is going on in this picture story by working out the number code. Each number matches a letter in the grid on the right hand page. Write the correct letter in the gaps to reveal the story. Some of the numbers are missing so you'll have to work out what those letters might be! Answer on page 30.

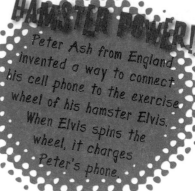

| 96 | 64 | 72 | 49 | | 22 | 64 | 72 |

___ ___ ___ ___   ___ ___ ___

| 89 | 82 | 67 | 85 | 86 | 38 |

Cummins ___ ___ ___ ___ ___ ___ moved

| 64 | 92 | 51 | 74 | 72 | | 22 | 64 | 72 | 38 |

___ ___ ___ ___ ___   ___ ___ ___ ___

| 86 | 92 | 74 | 22 | | 27 | 72 | 22 |

___ ___ ___ ___ their ___ ___ ___

| 64 | 82 | 67 | 74 | 22 | 72 | 68 |

___ ___ ___ ___ ___ ___ ___ .

Picture 1

Picture 2

| 82 | | 89 | 72 | 96 | | 86 | 82 | 22 | 72 | 68 |

___   ___ ___ ___   ___ ___ ___ ___ ___

___ ___ ___ ___ years ___ ___ ___ ___ ___

| 22 | 64 | 72 | 38 | | 82 | 84 | 82 | 85 | 49 |

___ ___ ___ ___ moved

| 82 | 49 | 29 | | 22 | 64 | 72 | 38 |

___ ___ ___   ___ ___ ___ ___ still hadn't

| 89 | 92 | 51 | 49 | 29 | | 22 | 64 | 72 | 85 | 68 |

___ ___ ___ ___ ___   ___ ___ ___ ___ ___

| 64 | 82 | 67 | 74 | 22 | 72 | 68 |

___ ___ ___ ___ ___ ___ ___ .

Picture 3

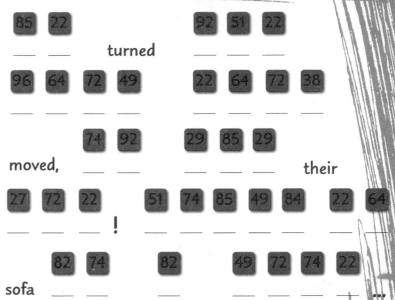

| 85 | 22 | | | | 92 | 51 | 22 |
| __ | __ | **turned** | | | __ | __ | __ |

| 96 | 64 | 72 | 49 | | 22 | 64 | 72 | 38 |
| __ | __ | __ | __ | | __ | __ | __ | __ |

| 74 | 92 | | 29 | 85 | 29 |
| **moved,** __ | __ | | **their** __ | __ | __ |

| 27 | 72 | 22 | | 51 | 74 | 85 | 49 | 84 | 22 | 64 | 72 |
| __ | __ | __ | **!** | __ | __ | __ | __ | __ | __ | __ | __ |

| 82 | 74 | | 82 | | 49 | 72 | 74 | 22 |
| **sofa** __ | __ | | __ | | __ | __ | __ | __ | **...** |

Picture 4

| 64 | 72 | | 64 | 82 | 29 | | 31 | 72 | 72 | 49 |
| **...** __ | __ | | __ | __ | __ | | __ | __ | __ | __ |

| 92 | 51 | 22 | | 82 | 22 |
| **sneaking** __ | __ | __ | | __ | __ | **night** |

| 22 | 92 | | 89 | 72 | 72 | 29 |
| __ | __ | | __ | __ | __ | __ |

| 89 | 68 | 92 | 67 | | 22 | 64 | 72 | 85 | 68 |
| __ | __ | __ | __ | | __ | __ | __ | __ | __ |

| 31 | 92 | 96 | 86 | 74 |
| **other pets'** __ | __ | __ | __ | __ | **.** |

A	B	C	D	E	F	G	H	I	J	K	L	M
82	31	55	29	72	89	84		85	43	79	86	67

N	O	P	Q	R	S	T	U	V	W	X	Y	Z
	92	27	60	68		22	51	77	96	99		53

11

FOOD FRIGHT

Sick of the same old boring meals? Don't be. There's plenty out there to eat, but it might not be what you're used to!

Match these freaky foods with the countries they're from. Answers on page 30.

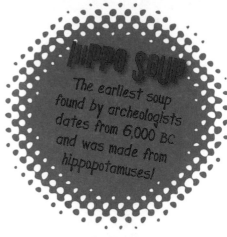

HIPPO SOUP
The earliest soup found by archeologists dates from 6,000 BC and was made from hippopotamuses!

CLUE
You might not want to start your meal with this...

China

CLUE
It's very smelly, but might be nice in your sandwich...

Italy

CLUE
It's a feast that has more than four legs...

Cambodia

CLUE
It's a liquid that's a little bit stinky...

Indonesia

Casu marzu
A cheese that wriggles with maggots!

Kopi luwak
Coffee made from cat's poo!

Bird's nest soup
Includes bird saliva!

Fried tarantulas
Nice and crunchy!

Ripley's— **Believe It or Not!**

BEAR ESCAPE

Juan, an Andean bear, was so desperate to escape from Berlin Zoo, Germany, that he came up with a complicated plan.

First, Juan used a log as a raft to float across the water around his enclosure.

Then, he heaved himself up over a high wall...

and found a bicycle. He may well have ridden off...

if he hadn't been calmed down with some tranquilizer darts and taken back to his home.

Help this bold bear dodge the lion and zookeepers to make it out of the maze.

FINISH

START

Answer on page 30

Ripley's—*Believe It or Not!*

WACKY RACES

These real-life crazy cars are certainly designed to stand out in traffic.

But, in this race, which one will make it to the finish line first? Follow their tracks to find out.

Turbo Beetle
Has a jet engine, but can it take corners?

Fish Car
Streamlined maybe, but will it "fin"-ish at all?

Peel car
Only 54 inches long, but that doesn't mean it isn't fast!

CRASH

BOOM

FINISH

CALL OF THE WILD

Did you know that there are between three million and 30 million species of animal on our planet?

That's a lot to choose from when answering this crossword's creature questions! Answers on page 30.

ACROSS

1. An animal with a long body that slithers along the floor. (5)

3. Often called "the king of the jungle." (4)

4. A giant African mammal that spends all day in the water. (5)

5. This sea-dwelling mammal is the largest creature that's ever lived. (5)

6. A striped wild cat that lives in the jungle and loves to swim. (5)

DOWN

2. The largest animal living on land now. (8)

4. Finish this phrase: "Eyes like a ....." Hint: it's a fast-flying bird of prey. (4)

7. One of the fiercest predators under the sea. (5)

Half tiger, half lion— what is this animal called? Write the answer below using the color code.

FAST TRACKER

Most sharks are slow swimmers, but the ferocious mako shark reaches top speeds of 55 mph!

FUN IN THE SUN

In Italy, pet dogs are not allowed on most beaches in summer, but Bau Beach near Rome spoils them rotten. Here, your beloved pooch can even get its own towel and umbrella!

Using the beach symbols already in place, complete each of the four grids so that every column, row and mini-grid only contains one of each picture.

See if you can find all of the symbols in the picture below!

Answers on page 31

BREAKFAST BREAK-IN

What would you do if you had an unwanted guest for breakfast? Not a human guest, but a big, hairy guest with claws and teeth!

Use the code at the bottom of the page to find out how one lady dealt with this beastly problem.

A woman in   had a huge fright when she walked into her

       and found a   eating

        ! The   was munching on

a   of

it had found, so the lady called the   .

It then took three   to remove the

      to safety.

Answer on page 31

A	B	C	D	E	F	G	H	I	J	K	L	M

N	O	P	Q	R	S	T	U	V	W	X	Y	Z

Ripley's—Believe It or Not!®

HUNGRY PENGUINS

When it's summer in the Antarctic, penguins often make a 100-mile trip across the ice to the open sea to feed. Then they turn around and attempt the dangerous journey home.

Start at their home at the bottom of the page and battle through the maze to the fish, avoiding the cracks in the ice. Then try to get back, but this time avoid the seals instead!

now it's time to eat!

Answer on page 31

HOME SWEET HOME!

TOP TIP!
Use different colors for the journey to the sea and the journey home again.

TEA TIME

LA Pop Art group created this picture of Alice's tea party by writing almost every word in Lewis Carroll's book *Alice in Wonderland* in different color pens. It shows Alice taking tea with the March Hare, Dormouse and the Mad Hatter.

Using the picture, answer the clues below to complete the crossword puzzle.

ACROSS

1. How many ears does the March Hare have? (3)

2. What color is the March Hare's bow tie? (4)

3. Which animal is sitting next to the March Hare? (8)

5. What color are the dots on the Mad Hatter's tie? (3)

7. What color is the chair Alice is sitting on? (5)

8. What type of hat is the Mad Hatter wearing? (3, 3)

DOWN

1. What is the March Hare pouring their drinks from? (6)

2. What color is Alice's hair? (5)

4. What are they drinking? (3)

6. How many cups are on the table? (5)

Answers on page 31

Ripley's — Believe *It or Not!* **19**

BEARS IN THE AIR

It was a giant leap for teddy bears everywhere when four teddies were blasted up into space. Wearing spacesuits designed by schoolchildren, the "teddynauts" parachuted safely back down to Earth after their outer space adventure.

Follow the wiggly lines to find out whether Teddy or Bear is safely attached to the spaceship. Then color them and the spaceship.

TRAVELING TRASH

From 1986 to 2001, the Mir space station threw 200 garbage bags into space, and they are still floating round the Earth right now.

METAL MONSTER

Robosaurus is a 40-foot-tall robotic dinosaur with a jaw seven times stronger than the real *T-Rex*! It can crush cars and planes, and shoot 20-foot flames from its nostrils.

Join the dots to discover what he looks like. Be afraid!

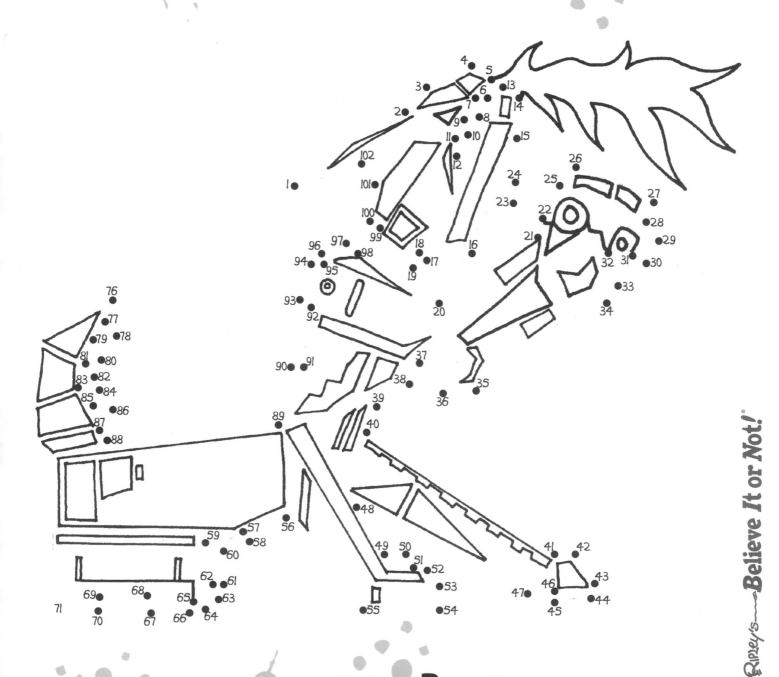

WHAT IS ROBOSAURUS HOLDING? _____

Space is full of unbelievable and amazing things. More are being discovered every year, too!

Work out the codes below, using the grid at the bottom of the page, to reveal what is happening in these spaced out stories.

1. In 2000, scientists   an

   ___ ___ ___ ___ ___   ___ ___ ___ ___ ___ ___ ___

   shaped like a   Maybe the star constellation

   ___ ___ ___ ___ ___ ___ ___ ___ ___.

   called the    would find it tasty.

   ___ ___ ___ ___ ___   ___ ___ ___

2.   created a giant   in 2009

   ___ ___ ___ ___   ___ ___ ___ ___ ___ ___   ___ ___ ___ ___

   to celebrate the 40th anniversary of the   moon landing.

   ___ ___ ___ ___ ___

   The special   consisted of marshmallow squeezed around two

   ___ ___ ___   ___ ___ ___ ___ ___

           and dipped in

   ___ ___ ___ ___ ___ ___ ___ ___   ___ ___ ___ ___ ___ ___ ___ ___

A	B	C	D	E	F	G	H	I	J	K	L	M

N	O	P	Q	R	S	T	U	V	W	X	Y	Z

CRAZY CUBE CODE

Ever tried to finish a Rubik's Cube? They can be tricky. Why not try our sudoku Rubik's Cube instead...

Using the colored squares already in place, complete the grids below so that each column and row, and each of the four smaller squares, only contain one of each color.

1

2

3

4

Answers on page 31

MOUNTAIN MEAL

What's the most amazing meal you've ever eaten? Maybe there was something about the food, the company or the view. Here's a tale that contains all three of those vital ingredients for perfect dining. Every picture represents a missing word—simply say what you see!

Write down what each symbol means in the spaces provided. If you get stuck for words, you can read the story in plain English on page 31.

BILL PLEASE! Raymond Salha and his wife were eating oysters in Lebanon when they discovered 26 pearls inside one of them!

The drinks were already chilled when six diners sat down for supper at a freezing -40°F.

The view was awesome because they were seated at 22,000 , just 7,000

_ _ _ _ _ _ _ _ _ _

below the summit of the 's highest —Mount Everest.

_ _ _ _ _ _ _ _ _

In May 2004, each dressed in a and formal wear, the climbers carried their

_ _ _ _ _ _ _ _ _

  and  up the slope. They also took a tablecloth,  ,

_ _ _ _ _ _ _ _ _ _ _ _ _

cutlery, wine glasses and even a candelabra! It was all part of their plan to enjoy the 's highest

_ _ _ _ _ _ _ _

formal dinner. The friends sat down to a four-course meal of caviar, smoked , and

_ _ _ _ _ _ _

 pudding, followed by a selection.

_ _ _ _ _ _ _ _ _ _ _ _

It's not the highest meal ever. In June 2005, Grylls hosted the highest freestanding dinner

_ _ _ _ _

party at a table suspended below a at 24,500 feet.

_ _ _ _ _ _ _ _ _ _ _ _

Ripley's——Believe It or Not!®

WITH A TWIST

Octi the octopus lives in an aquarium in New Zealand. Unbelievably, he uses his tentacles to open jars to get the food inside.

These five squares have been taken from the picture of Octi. Some of them have been given a twist, too! Find them on the grid and, underneath each one, write down their co-ordinates. We have given you the first answer, to show you how it's done. Answers on page 31.

(F, 4) ....

HIPPO HOUSEMATE

Imagine sharing your home with a one-ton teenage hippo who eats up to 175 pounds of food a day!

That was the task facing the South African couple who took on an unusual orphan over ten years ago. Park ranger Tonie Joubert and his wife Shirley discovered the baby hippo alone on the banks of a river when she was just a few hours old. At that age, she weighed only 35 pounds.

Jessica—found alone on the banks of a river.

She had been swept away from her mother in devastating floods that hit South Africa and Mozambique in 2000. Knowing that wild hippos stay with their mothers for at least four years, the Jouberts decided to take her home, and called her Jessica.

They gave the young hippo heavy-duty massages and allowed her to wander about the house before she grew really big, breaking beds in the house three times!

Over time, Jessica moved out to join the wild hippos that visit the Joubert home, but she still lives close by her adopted family. When they return from a trip they often find her waiting by the house for a meal. Jessica sometimes eats in the house—she's allowed in the kitchen and the lounge—and drinks more than 2½ gallons of coffee a day!

Relaxing after just 2½ gallons of coffee!

Ripley's—Believe It or Not!®

Now test your knowledge about Jessica by answering the questions below. Fill them in on the crossword, then turn to page 31 to see if you're right!

oops!

This bed ain't big enough!

Remember not to talk with your mouth full!

Down

1. Name one of the rooms in the house where Jessica is still allowed to go. (7)

2. In which country does Jessica live now? (5, 6)

4. Which of her relatives had Jessica been separated from almost from birth? (6)

5. What does Jessica drink 2½ gallons of each day? (6)

Across

3. What is "hippo" the shortened term for? (12)

6. What piece of furniture did Jessica break three times? (3)

7. How many years do young hippos usually stay with their mothers? (4)

8. What did the Jouberts give Jessica when she first came to stay? (8)

CREATURE CODE

A secret code is a brilliant way to pass on a message without everyone being able to read it. Use the code at the bottom of the page to unravel some important animal information.

Check you cracked the codes correctly on page 31.

1. When a  has found good

 it flies back to the

and starts  By running and

, the tells the others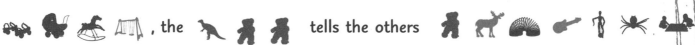

where to  the

_ .

2. Which animal sleeps with one eye open and one eye closed?

_ _ _ _ _ _ _ _ _ _ _ _ _ .

A	B	C	D	E	F	G	H	I	J	K	L	M
N	O	P	Q	R	S	T	U	V	W	X	Y	Z

Ripley's — Believe It or Not!®

SLOW START

Every year, the official World Snail Racing Championship takes place in England. Snails slime their way from the center of a circle to the edge. Blink and you won't miss it!

Sidney, Rocket Man and his friends are slugging it out in the race below, but which snail finishes in which place? Follow the paths to find out and write the results in the boxes, adding the champion racer at the bottom of the page.

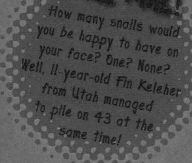

WHO WON?

ANSWERS

SPORTS MAD PAGE 3

HOMER'S D'OH-NUT PAGE 5

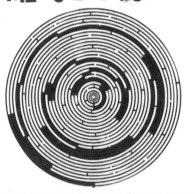

PECKER PUZZLE PAGE 6

Scientists found that hungry woodpeckers had pecked over 200 holes in the foam insulation on the space shuttle Discovery's fuel tank. So, a NASA worker bought 6 plastic owls to scare them away!

BRUSH UP! PAGE 8

1,800 types of toothpaste

CRAZY CAT CIRCUS PAGE 9

mouse!

ON THE MOVE PAGES 10–11

Picture 1
When the Cummins family moved house they lost their pet hamster.

Picture 2
A few years later they moved again and they still hadn't found their hamster.

Picture 3
It turned out when they moved, so did their pet! Using the sofa as a nest...

Picture 4
...he had been sneaking out at night to feed from their other pets' bowls.

FOOD FRIGHT PAGE 12

Fried tarantulas = **Cambodia**

Kopi luwak = **Indonesia**

Bird's nest soup = **China**

Casu marzu = **Italy**

BEAR ESCAPE PAGE 13

CALL OF THE WILD PAGE 15

FUN IN THE SUN PAGE 16

BREAKFAST BREAK-IN PAGE 17

A woman in **Canada** had a huge fright when she walked into her **kitchen** and found a **bear** eating **porridge**! The **bear** was munching on a **container** of oatmeal it had found, so lady called the **police**. It then took three **officers** to remove the **animal** to safety.

HUNGRY PENGUINS PAGE 18

The red line shows their journey to eat.

The blue line shows their journey back home.

TEA TIME PAGE 19

```
              ¹T W O
        ²B L U E   A
        L         P
        O    ³D O R M O U S E   ⁴T
     ⁵R ⁶E D    T            E
        I                    A
        ⁷G R E E N
        H
        ⁸T O P H A T
```

METAL MONSTER PAGE 21

Robosaurus is holding a car

WE HAVE LIFT OFF! PAGE 22

1. In 2000, scientists **found** an **asteroid** shaped like a **dog bone**. Maybe the star constellation called the **Great Dog** would find it tasty.

2. **Nasa** created a giant **moon pie** in 2009 to celebrate the 40th anniversary of the **first** moon landing. The special **pie** consisted of marshmallow squeezed around two **giant crackers** and dipped in **chocolate**.

CRAZY CUBE CODE PAGE 23

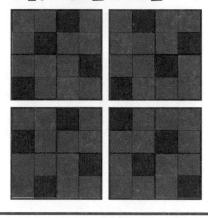

MOUNTAIN MEAL PAGE 24

The drinks were already chilled when six diners sat down for supper at a freezing -4OF. The view was awesome because they were seated at 22,000 **feet**, just 7,000 **feet** below the summit of the **world's** highest **mountain**—Mount Everest. In May 2004, each dressed in a **top hat** and formal wear, the climbers carried their **chairs** and **tables** up the slope. They also took a tablecloth, **plates**, cutlery, wine glasses and even a candelabra! It was all part of their plan to enjoy the **world's** highest formal dinner.

The friends sat down to a four-course meal of caviar, smoked **duck**, and **chocolate** pudding, followed by a **cheese** selection.

It's not the highest meal ever. In June 2005, **Bear** Grylls hosted the highest freestanding dinner party at a table suspended below a **hot air balloon** at 24,500 feet.

WITH A TWIST PAGE 25

(F, 4) (E, 3) (D, 1) (A, 3) (B, 2)

HIPPO HOUSEMATE PAGES 26-27

```
           ¹K      ²S
        ³H I P P O P O T A ⁴M U S
           T      U       O
           C      T   ⁵C  T
           H      H   O   H
        ⁶B E D    A   F   E
           N      F   ⁷F O U R
                  R   E
                  I   E
                  C
              ⁸M A S S A G E S
```

CREATURE CODE PAGE 28

1. When a **honeybee** has found good **flowers** it flies back to the **hive** and starts **dancing**. By running **up** and **down**, the **bee** tells the others **exactly** where to **find** the **flowers**.

2. Which animal sleeps with one eye open and one eye closed?
   A dolphin.

RIPLEY
PUBLISHING

Cartoons drawn by Ripley's resident cartoonist
John Graziano

Written, designed and illustrated by
Rosie Alexander, Michelle Foster, Charlotte Howell,
Becky Miles, Lisa Regan, Sam South

Reprographics
Juice Creative

ISBN: 978-1-60991-088-4

For information regarding permission, write to
VP Intellectual Property, Ripley Entertainment Inc.
Suite 188, 7576 Kingspointe Parkway
Orlando, Florida 32819

Email: publishing@ripleys.com

Manufactured in Dallas, PA, United States
in March/2013 by Offset Paperback Manufacturers
1st printing

PUBLISHER'S NOTE
While every effort has been made to verify the accuracy of the facts in this
book, the Publishers cannot be held responsible for any errors contained in
the work. They would be glad to receive any information from readers.

WARNING
Some of the stunts and activities in this book are undertaken
by experts and should not be attempted by anyone without
adequate training and supervision.